BLESSED IS THE MAN WHO TRUSTS IN THE LORD

For he will be like a tree planted by the water

25 DEVOTIONS FOR MEN

Kenneth Wagener

Blessed Is the Man Who Trusts in the Lord
by Kenneth Wagener

www.CTAinc.com

Copyright © 2007 CTA, Inc.
1625 Larkin Williams Rd.
Fenton, MO 63026-1205

Scripture quotations are from the King James or Authorized Version of the bible.

ISBN 978-1-933234-38-0

PRINTED IN THAILAND

Blessed is the man that trusteth in the LORD,
and whose hope the LORD is.
For he shall be as a tree planted by the waters,
and that spreadeth out her roots by the river.

Jeremiah 17:7–8

Through faith, God promises, you are blessed. He has
poured out his grace on you, and he now considers
you his beloved son because of the death and resurrection
of Jesus Christ.

Look at yourself as a man of faith whose life goal is to be a
mighty tree planted in the fertile, well-watered soil of God's love.
That's how Jeremiah describes you in the verses above. That's good
news as you live as a Christian in your family, daily work,
community, and church.

Start your devotional time each day with this prayer. Reflect on
how your Lord has called you. And to cultivate your growth in
his Word, read and pray about the Scripture passage in
"Deeper and Higher."

A Prayer Based on Jeremiah 17:7–8

Lord, you call me blessed. And so I am.
Call me your son again now, as I rest in your
fatherly care and *begin/end* this day.

Lord, I pray for myself . . . Plant me firmly in rich soil as I trust in
you. Let my roots go out far and wide, so that I may stand tall as a
man of faith in your world. Let my confidence in your Word grow
deeper and higher as you ground me in your truth and establish
me in your love. I especially ask . . . *Pray the Lord's guidance
on your beliefs and attitudes, your character, your talents
and skills, your management of his gifts, and your service
to his church.*

Lord, I pray for others . . . May they thrive in faith, growing
green leaves and plentiful fruit, even in the hot, dry seasons
of life. I especially ask . . . *Pray God's strength and wisdom for
your family, for all your relationships, for work and neighborhood
commitments, and for your witness to Christ.*

Lord, I pray for your help in a day of trouble . . . *Pray God's grace
and healing for temptation and pressure to conform, for loss and
hardships, for health concerns and conflict resolution, for yourself
and others.*

Make me stand strong and sturdy, Lord. Grow me every day in
your grace, as I bless your holy name. Amen.

Blessed is the man that trusteth in the LORD,
and whose hope the LORD is.
Jeremiah 17:7

God has planted you.

You are the tree of his choosing,
   the man he has designed
   and called you to be.

He is growing you deeper and higher,
   that you may be blessed and
   that he may be glorified in everything,
   to the praise and honor of Jesus Christ.

The Planter

And the LORD God planted a garden eastward in Eden; and there he put the man whom he had formed. (Genesis 2:8)

How did those tulip oak trees come to stand in the middle of your yard? How did that grove of cedars come to rim your property?

Most likely you planted them. Or perhaps the developer who created your subdivision. Then again, perhaps they grew tall and straight long before you—or anyone else—purchased your home or acreage and moved in. Even then, the truth is that someone planted those trees.

You know who! Your God. Your God is a planter. *The* planter of all creation. Don't miss the grace and power of God's character in the opening chapters of Scripture. In Genesis 1, God creates. God separates. God gathers. God causes trees and plants to grow. God crafts lights in the sky. God fashions and sends forth fish and birds and mammals. God creates it all—everything you see in this vast, magnificent planet called Earth.

And then the climax of his creation: "And the LORD God planted a garden eastward in Eden; and there he put the man whom he had formed." A perfect conclusion to the work of his hands. God is the master gardener.

Take another look at God the planter. He's planted you. Put you right where he wants you to stand, right where he wants you to mature. Placed you right where he wants to use you for his purposes. Your Father has created you and re-created you in Jesus Christ to be "the man that trusteth in the LORD, and whose hope the LORD is" (Jeremiah 17:7).

The devotional readings in this book will guide you into the prophet Jeremiah's faithful words from the Lord to you, the man he has formed by his perfect plan. Each day you'll explore the grace and power of God's presence and purpose in your life. You'll discover how God is calling and equipping you to be a tree rooted and refreshed in his love in Christ.

He's planted you to be evergreen and bear fruit. You are blessed!

Deeper and Higher
Consider how God looks at you:

They might be called trees of righteousness,
the planting of the LORD,
that he might be glorified.
Isaiah 61:3

Planted for His Blessing

And God said, Let us make man in our image, after our likeness: and let them have dominion over the fish of the sea, and over the fowl of the air, and over the cattle, and over all the earth, and over every creeping thing that creepeth upon the earth. (Genesis 1:26)

Have you noticed? The Bible honors you as God's special creation. As he did with Adam, your Father made you individually. He fashioned you uniquely in his divine image and likeness and set you apart as his representative, his delegate in his world. You, too, have authority to rule over the work of his hands.

But something else marks you as God's special creation. With fire in his heart and mind, Jeremiah declares, "Blessed is the man that trusteth in the LORD, and whose hope the LORD is" (17:7).

You are doubly blessed. God has made you alive again. He has re-created you for a new and living relationship with himself. He has refashioned your sinful self by grace and now shaped you into the image and likeness of his perfect Son, Jesus Christ. Through Jesus you now believe in our Creator God, and your confidence rests in the Father who richly and daily forgives, renews, and empowers you to live as a man of faith in your world. As a man of faith in all your relationships. As a man of faith in all your work.

You are a man who trusts in the Lord. And he has planted you to be a blessing to your world—to all the people he has planted in your life.

What will you invest in your relationships today? Think deeply about honoring the people close to your heart—a spouse, a parent, a son or daughter, or a friend. Ask your Father for insight and wisdom. Then thank him for the people he has placed in your life.

Deeper and Higher
Remember that God is making you new today—individually and in your relationship with others:

Lie not one to another, seeing that ye have put off the old man with his deeds; And have put on the new man, which is renewed in knowledge after the image of him that created him.
Colossians 3:9–10

Planting the Future

*For I know the thoughts that I think toward you, saith the LORD,
thoughts of peace, and not of evil, to give you an expected end.
(Jeremiah 29:11)*

Planting is an act of faith. You plant, believing that today is not
the end. You trust that tomorrow will arrive and bring new life
and new beginnings.

Jeremiah wrote a letter to God's people in exile in Babylon.
They'd been taken from their homeland by an enemy king.
Now they asked hard, troubling questions: Why go on?
Why do anything today when we don't know about tomorrow?

Through his prophet, God answered Israel: "Build ye houses,
and dwell in them; and plant gardens, and eat the fruit of them;
Take ye wives, and beget sons and daughters; and take wives for
your sons, and give your daughters to husbands, that they may
bear sons and daughters; that ye may be increased there,
and not diminished" (Jeremiah 29:5–6).

God was planting his tomorrow. He planted through the
children and grandchildren of this generation. He had plans
for his people—"thoughts of peace, and not of evil,
to give you an expected end" (29:11).

Are you planting hope and a future in your children? Or in the lives of children around you—nephews and nieces, grandsons and granddaughters, the boys and girls in your neighborhood or church?

Think back to the men who have shaped and mentored you in the past. They planted seeds—seeds of faith, hope, love—in your mind and heart. They cultivated a harvest—a harvest of goodness, gentleness, and other fruit of the Spirit—in your life. They invested in your today so that you might pass on a spiritual legacy for someone else's tomorrow.

What lasting things will you plant today, trusting the Lord to make them grow?

Deeper and Higher
God's reminder to you:

Behold, the husbandman waiteth for the precious fruit
of the earth, and hath long patience for it,
until he receive the early and latter rain.
Be ye also patient; stablish your hearts.
James 5:7–8

Planting with Purpose

So then neither is he that planteth any thing, neither he that watereth; but God that giveth the increase. Now he that planteth and he that watereth are one: and every man shall receive his own reward according to his own labour. (1 Corinthians 3:7–8)

Buyouts. Outsourcing. Downsizing. These are the words that describe today's workplaces.

Years ago, most jobs had the life cycle of trees. You were planted on a farm or in a factory or at an office. You grew there; you flowered and ripened and retired where—or close to where—you began. But not so today.

Even if you are relatively young in your career, you've likely been uprooted and replanted at least once. Or trimmed back. Or perhaps you feel like you've been cut down and tossed aside to make room for other trees—younger, fresher, more colorful or distinctive. Maybe you're no longer firmly rooted, and you're restless to find a workplace where you can sink your roots down deep and begin—more securely and consistently—to bear fruit.

What meaning does work have in today's competitive, global economy? What meaning does *your* work have? Does it mean anything at all? God says, Yes! Your work has purpose—whatever it is—because God has called you to it. 1 Peter 4:10 tells us, "As every man hath received the gift, even so minister the same one to another." He is working through you. He is working with you and in you to make his world grow and flourish.

As you go about your daily tasks, varied as they may be, you are planting and watering. You work, but ultimately God gives the growth. He has planned your work—past, present, and future—and he promises to give you the wisdom and strength you need to carry out his purposes for you.

You can trust your Father to guide you as you go about your tasks today. You can call on him for focus and drive when you meet challenges and setbacks. Then watch him bless the results as you put your confidence in Christ.

Deeper and Higher
Stand firm in the promise God makes to you:

*Be ye stedfast, unmoveable, always abounding
in the work of the Lord, forasmuch as ye know
that your labour is not in vain in the Lord.*
1 Corinthians 15:58

Planting Better Together

Two are better than one; because they have a good reward for their labour. For if they fall, the one will lift up his fellow: but woe to him that is alone when he falleth; for he hath not another to help him up. (Ecclesiastes 4:9–10)

What do you like to do with your friends?

Golf?
Fish or hunt?
Visit car shows or take motorcycle trips?
Attend NASCAR races or use season tickets to your favorite pro team's games?
Joke by e-mail or text messaging?

Solomon pictures friends doing something more. In his pointed meditation on life (the book in the Bible named Ecclesiastes), Israel's wise king sees men working side by side, planting, harvesting, building, tearing down, scattering, gathering, waging war, pursuing peace—the whole range of human activities under the sun.

All this happens, he notes, by God's design. The Father sets a season for everything (Ecclesiastes 3:1), and he gives men— young and old—the grace and skill to accomplish all their tasks.

Yet "two are better than one." Friends stand together. Friends succeed together. Friends defend themselves together. Friends do together—better together—what they cannot do alone.

Your friends are a gift to you from your Father. He has planted them in your life, perhaps next door, perhaps across the state or country. Wherever they are, God brought you together so that your life—and your faith—would be stronger, richer, more influential than the life you could live "on your own."

The Lord has plans for you and your friends. He wants you to grow—together—to be men of faith, cheering one another on, urging one another upward in the call to live in service to Christ and his church.

Take time for your friends today. Do something! And rest in the confidence that your Father will bless you in it as you grow.

Deeper and Higher
Meditate on your Savior's words of affirmation:

I have called you friends; for all things that I have heard of my Father I have made known unto you. Ye have not chosen me, but I have chosen you, and ordained you, that ye should go and bring forth fruit, and that your fruit should remain: that whatsoever ye shall ask of the Father in my name, he may give it you. These things I command you, that ye love one another.
John 15:15–17

Who Am I?

Over the next two days, reflect on the different ways
God is working in your life to draw you closer to himself in
faith and to bless you to be a blessing to others.

My Identity as a Man
My Relationships
The Children in My Life
My Work
My Friends

Blessed is the man that trusteth in the LORD,
and whose hope the LORD *is.*
Jeremiah 17:7

For he shall be as a tree planted by the waters,
and that spreadeth out her roots by the river.
Jeremiah 17:8

God has planted you in Christ.

Every day he draws you to the Living Water,
who alone will satisfy your thirsty soul.

Let your roots spread out, far and wide,
    as you recognize his blessings in your life.

Set apart the gifts he has entrusted to you,
    and dedicate yourself
    to growing deeper and higher in his Word,
    that all may see Jesus in you.

Roots

Rooted and built up in him, and stablished in the faith,
as ye have been taught, abounding therein with thanksgiving.
(Colossians 2:7)

Go underground. Subterranean. That's where you'll find roots.

Below every grand and sturdy tree, you'll find a remarkable
system of roots. Sprawling, twisting, and hidden, roots play vital
roles in the life of a tree. Roots anchor the trunk and branches.
Roots provide stability when winter winds bluster. Roots absorb
nutrients—oxygen and minerals—from the soil. Roots store
food—carbohydrates—produced by the tree. Who cares about
roots? Only wise and diligent gardeners.

Jeremiah describes you when he writes, "He shall be as a tree
planted by the waters, and that spreadeth out her roots by the
river" (Jeremiah 17:8). God planted you, and now he desires that
you set down roots to anchor and nourish and preserve you as
you carry out the work he has in mind for you to do. Think for a
moment about your roots—that sprawling, twisting, hidden
system of deep beliefs, principles, and attitudes. How would
you describe them? In what ways do your roots anchor and
nurture you? Now listen to the apostle Paul:

For in him dwelleth all the fulness of the Godhead bodily. And ye are complete in him, which is the head of all principality and power. (Colossians 2:9–10)

You have fullness in Jesus. True God, true man, Christ continually fills you with his life—his crucifixion and resurrection life. He begins that filling at the roots. He begins with the beliefs, principles, and attitudes that flow from your deepest identity as his forgiven, precious son. As you seek him in his Word, you absorb his sacrificial love, his unsurpassed wisdom and truth, his passion for lost men.

Think of Jesus as the wise and diligent gardener who cultivates you to make you strong and overflowing with thankfulness. Let him do his work in you today, his subterranean work.

Deeper and Higher
As you pray today, ask that the Father:

grant you, according to the riches of his glory, to be strengthened with might by his Spirit in the inner man; That Christ may dwell in your hearts by faith; that ye, being rooted and grounded in love, May be able to comprehend with all saints what is the breadth, and length, and depth, and height; And to know the love of Christ, which passeth knowledge, that ye might be filled with all the fulness of God.
Ephesians 3:16–19

Noble Character

These were more noble than those in Thessalonica, in that they received the word with all readiness of mind, and searched the scriptures daily, whether those things were so. (Acts 17:11)

Maybe you've said it at some point: "That tree has character!"

Some trees stand out from the rest. You notice their unusual shape. Their vibrant colors. Or their intriguing pattern of branches. Trees have *character*. Look closely and you'll discern the qualities and traits that make each one distinctive, each one significant.

For Jeremiah, the "tree planted by the waters" has its own cluster of qualities and traits—a character that comes directly from God. The Lord forms it. The Lord shapes it, giving it the exact contour and profile he wishes. God knows what it takes to bring out the vibrant colors. He understands how to cultivate its true character and make it flourish, how to generate ample, sturdy branches. The Lord knows just exactly how he will use this tree to impact his world.

Look closely to discern how God is forming your character as well. You may struggle with relationships at the office. You may worry about retirement years and financial security for your future. You may wrestle with sexual temptations and the call to purity. You may wonder how to communicate with the woman you love.

Through all these challenges, God seeks to shape the true you, to make it possible for you to express outwardly the new inward character he has given you in Christ. His work begins, as the Bereans understood, in his Word.

Through his Word, your Father will make you the distinctive tree he wants you to be. In that Word he reveals your true significance, your true identity as his beloved son, connected in faith to the Beloved Son, Jesus Christ.

As you read and hear the Scriptures, receive God's message with "all readiness of mind." Open your Bible "daily" to feed the roots of your faith. Let your Father use his Word to shape your character—your noble character in Christ—so that others around you may know his Word is true.

Deeper and Higher

Be confident in the Lord's promise:

*He which hath begun a good
work in you will perform
it until the day of
Jesus Christ.*
Philippians 1:6

One Treasure

Godliness with contentment is great gain. (1 Timothy 6:6)

Godliness? Certainly. Contentment with one's possessions? Yes, but hard to do in our materialistic society. Both in the same breath? Wow! What a juxtaposition!

Some say, "Let's keep faith and finances in separate corners. Let's put our heavenly riches and our earthly wallets in different back pockets. What God gives us spiritually and what we earn by the sweat of our brow are two unrelated matters." Right?

The man who trusts in the Lord recognizes all God's gifts—including money—as blessings from his hands. A tree planted by water, with roots deep and wide in God's grace, receives God's daily goodness with a spirit of thanksgiving and contentment.

But how about you? Do you trust God with your money? Do you know his will for your finances? As Paul the apostle writes to Timothy, he shares some profound convictions about money and wealth. Ponder the insights he shares as he closes his letter (1 Timothy 6:17–19):

- Though you may be rich in this present world, don't be arrogant or put your hope in earthly wealth. It's all uncertain; you have no guarantee you'll have anything tomorrow—or that you'll be on earth to need it!
- God richly provides us with everything for our enjoyment. He opens his heart and hands and freely gives. Take! Enjoy! Use responsibly.

- Do good with what you have, be rich in good deeds, and share generously and willingly. You demonstrate the goodness and generosity of Christ as you help others in need.
- Lay up treasure in heaven, for God has planned your true life with him forever.

By trusting God with your money and finances, you send your roots out far and wide into the fertile soil of thanksgiving and contentment. Whatever comes, you trust your Father will care for you, will provide for you and those you love most.

God gives you one wallet, one pocket . . . to hold everything he gives. All his blessings belong in the same pocket because, after all, it's all one treasure, one pure gift from your heavenly Father. Thank him today for his kindness.

Deeper and Higher

Remember the treasure that Jesus has poured out on you:

For ye know the grace of our Lord Jesus Christ, that, though he was rich, yet for your sakes he became poor, that ye through his poverty might be rich.
2 Corinthians 8:9

Useful to the Master

Bless, LORD, his substance, and accept the work of his hands.
(Deuteronomy 33:11)

At the end of his life Moses prayed for his people—for the
Israelites. One by one, tribe after tribe, this man of God offered
brief yet heartfelt prayers for the men, women, and children he
had traveled and lived with from slavery in Egypt to the brink of
the Promised Land. Now his death was in sight; time was short.
So he turned to his Father to ask a blessing for generations
to come.

"Bless, LORD, his substance," Moses prayed. "Accept the work
of his hands."

What skills has God given you? Whatever they are, first
recognize them as his gifts. Your talents, your abilities and
expertise, learned or natural, all derive from your Father. All
your skills, whatever you have, all have come to you unearned,
simply by God's grace to you. He has planted them in you, like
different kinds of trees in a yard, and has caused each to thrive
as you have needed them.

But also be sure to see your skills as tools—God-given tools. You
build with tools. You fix with tools. You modify and fine-tune
and make things better and more durable with tools.

God uses your skills as tools for his purposes. And he gives you the privilege of offering whatever tools you have—some sharp, some rusty—as the work of your hands to honor him and serve the people he has placed in your life.

Recall again Jeremiah's words: "Blessed is the man that trusteth in the LORD, and whose hope the LORD is" (17:7). Your trust, your confidence are anchored in the Lord. Why not pray that the Lord bless your skills and the work of your hands—for his glory and purposes? Why not pray for your family, your co-workers, your friends and neighbors, that their skills also may be channeled in service to the Lord?

And ask your Father also for work—tool work!—work that will please him and will build and fix and improve your home life and workplace and neighborhood and church. Let him work through you to richly bless others.

Deeper and Higher
Know that you serve the only King.

Seest thou a man diligent in his business?
he shall stand before kings.
Proverbs 22:29

Gifts of the Spirit

That in every thing ye are enriched by him, in all utterance, and in all knowledge; So that ye come behind in no gift; waiting for the coming of our Lord Jesus Christ. (1 Corinthians 1:5, 7)

Jesus gives gifts to his church. Raised to heaven and ruling over this vast universe, the Lord pours out of heaven's abundance upon his people. The Bible makes it doubly certain. David predicted it, and Paul announced its fulfillment: "When he ascended up on high, he led captivity captive, and gave gifts unto men" (Ephesians 4:8; see also Psalm 68:18).

Each gift of grace, bestowed and empowered by the Holy Spirit, flows from the crucified and risen Lord. Forgiveness. Peace. Joy. Purpose in life. Comfort in times of pain and loss. Fellowship in the body of Christ. Brotherhood with Christ himself!

In addition to all this, Jesus has also given you spiritual gifts—not just attitudes and skills, but supernatural abilities—to be used to support and unify the body of Christ and to reach beyond the body to grow the Kingdom:

Now there are diversities of gifts, but the same Spirit. And there are differences of administrations, but the same Lord. And there are diversities of operations, but it is the same God which worketh all in all. (1 Corinthians 12:4–6)

Your Father has planted these gifts in you and in all other believers. He gives these gifts graciously, without measure. And he wants the gifts he has planted in you to grow. Be bold, then, to call on him to broaden and sharpen his gifts. You are a man of confidence. Christ dwells in you by faith. Ask him to enrich your thinking, speaking, and doing, confident that you lack nothing as you serve him until he returns in glory.

Deeper and Higher
Rest assured in, and be motivated to serve by,
the Spirit's gift to you and all Christians:

But all these worketh that one and the selfsame Spirit, dividing to every man severally as he will.
1 Corinthians 12:11

God @ Work

*During these next two days, reflect on the different ways
God is working in your life to draw you closer to him
in faith and bless you to be a blessing to others.*

My Attitudes
My Character
My Finances
My Skills
My Spiritual Gifts

*For he shall be as a tree planted by the waters,
and that spreadeth out her roots by the river.*
Jeremiah 17:8

Blessed is the man that trusteth in the LORD, and whose hope the LORD is. For he shall be as a tree planted by the waters, and that spreadeth out her roots by the river, and shall not see when heat cometh, but her leaf shall be green.
Jeremiah 17:7–8

God has planted you for every season.
Though you may feel burned,
       scorched by the pressures
       of this fallen, sinful world,
       don't be afraid; you are not alone.

Your Lord has chosen you
       and called you to be a man of faith,
       trusting in his guidance and protection.

He will equip you,
       growing you deeper and higher,
       that you may stand against the heat
       and flourish in his grace.

Conformed to the Son

As obedient children, not fashioning yourselves according to the former lusts in your ignorance: But as he which hath called you is holy, so be ye holy in all manner of conversation; Because it is written, Be ye holy; for I am holy. (1 Peter 1:14–16)

Trees can wither when temperatures soar. Young trees, not yet fully formed, are especially vulnerable when the heat is on. Without plentiful water and relief from blistering sunlight, even mature trees can languish.

God calls you to be a "tree planted by the waters." Yet he knows you live and move and have your being in this fallen, sinful world. At times, the pressures to conform to the pattern of this world can overwhelm even mature Christians. The temptations of a world system broken and hostile to its creator can blister our souls and wilt our resolve.

Internet pornography. The temptation to cut corners at the office or in the shop. The belief that only those who compromise their principles get ahead. The frustrations inherent in accountability. The busy-ness that kills relationships. A critical attitude toward our children or others we mentor at home, church, or work. The list might soar into the hundreds . . .

When you feel the heat, the pressure to conform, what do you do? Do you turn to the cool, refreshing Living Water . . . Jesus Christ? If so, you need not fear when the heat comes. You have been grafted by grace onto his tree—his cross. You have been united with him in his life—the new life of his resurrection. You stand in the shade of his forgiveness, and you are daily rejuvenated—made whole, fresh, and green because of his mercy and love.

When the temperature rises in your life, your Father invites you into the seasonable weather of his promises in Christ. Stay close to him. Let the Lord conform you to his image for you—a mature, evergreen tree, seeking his holy will.

Deeper and Higher
Hear your God's call:

And be not conformed to this world: but be ye
transformed by the renewing of your mind,
that ye may prove what is that good,
and acceptable, and perfect, will of God.
Romans 12:2

The Servant Way

Let nothing be done through strife or vainglory; but in lowliness of mind let each esteem other better than themselves. Look not every man on his own things, but every man also on the things of others. (Philippians 2:3–4)

Ancient peoples had a ready label for harsh, oppressive, unjust rulers: **tyrants!**

Tyranny was the rule of the ruler. What the ruler says, goes. What the ruler wants, he gets. No limitations. No boundaries. No checks and balances on his quest for power, authority, and greatness . . . none, that is, until another tyrant, more crafty and ruthless, comes along. Then the tyranny starts all over again.

Sometimes the heat of battle creates tyrants. Men fall prey to tyranny—their own. They issue orders. They make demands. They take what they want, when they want it, without considering the consequences of their actions and the damage they leave in their wake. They become dictators.

"Not so among you," Jesus encouraged his disciples. James and John, perhaps the other men too, had jockeyed for position— powerful, authoritative, and great positions—in Jesus' kingdom. But they missed the heart and character of his rule. Dwell on the Lord's words:

But so shall it not be among you: but whosoever will be great among you, shall be your minister: And whosoever of you will be the chiefest, shall be servant of all. For even the Son of man came not to be ministered unto, but to minister, and to give his life a ransom for many. (Mark 10:43–45)

You may have power. You may have authority. You may be well positioned for status and reward in the future. But remember your Lord's call: minister . . . servant . . . "came not to be ministered unto, but to minister."

When the heat is on—to succeed at work, to finish projects at home, to make a difference in Little League baseball—you'll need the servant's attitude more than ever. The temptation will be tyranny. But ask your Father for the heart and character of his Son. Listen to your Savior. Learn from Christ's servant way. Invite him to rain down his grace to grow you as one who serves.

Deeper and Higher
An attitude check for the man of God:

Let this mind be in you, which was also in Christ Jesus: Who, being in the form of God, thought it not robbery to be equal with God: But made himself of no reputation, and took upon him the form of a servant.
Philippians 2:5–7

Day 17

Spiritual Desires

For they that are after the flesh do mind the things of the flesh; but they that are after the Spirit the things of the Spirit. (Romans 8:5)

C. S. Lewis once wrote, "Every time you make a choice you are turning the central part of you, the part that chooses, into something a little different from what it was before."

The pressures of this world knock daily at your sinful nature. Anyone home? The reality is *yes*. Inside you, as the apostle Paul describes, is a residue, leftovers of sorts, of the man you once were. The apostle Paul reminds us, "For there is no difference: For all have sinned, and come short of the glory of God" (Romans 3:22–23). That was your identity. That describes the man you were before the lavish, transforming grace of your Father in the gift of his Son.

Before: *There is none righteous, no, not one: There is none that understandeth, there is none that seeketh after God. They are all gone out of the way, they are together become unprofitable. (Romans 3:10–12)*

After: *Know ye not, that so many of us as were baptized into Jesus Christ were baptized into his death? Therefore we are buried with him by baptism into death: that like as Christ was raised up from the dead by the glory of the Father, even so we also should walk in newness of life. (Romans 6:3–4)*

Within you, just as within every other Christian who has ever lived, the new, Spirit-given nature battles with the old, sin-stained nature. And the Spirit is serious! He desires to draw you to Christ. He wills to plant you firmly in the Word so that by his Spirit alive in every part of you—roots, trunk, branches, even leaves—you bear abundant fruit. He wants every choice you make to turn you away from the old, sinful nature and toward a higher, deeper relationship with your Lord.

Ask your Father today to renew your desires so that they reflect the Holy Spirit's desires. He will help you choose new life.

Deeper and Higher
Ready to follow? Fall in step with the Spirit:

But the fruit of the Spirit is love, joy, peace, longsuffering, gentleness, goodness, faith, Meekness, temperance: against such there is no law. And they that are Christ's have crucified the flesh with the affections and lusts.
Galatians 5:22–24

A New Leaf

Put on therefore, as the elect of God, holy and beloved, bowels of mercies, kindness, humbleness of mind, meekness, longsuffering; Forbearing one another, and forgiving one another, if any man have a quarrel against any: even as Christ forgave you, so also do ye. (Colossians 3:12–13)

You get burned in a relationship. Someone scorches you at work. What do you feel? White-hot anger!

Heat seems to go naturally with anger. When the heat's on, how do you respond? Do you rage inside? Do you inwardly simmer and boil with resentment and hatred, waiting for the right moment to let off steam? Or do you blow your top and pour down rivers of molten lava—words and actions—that threaten to consume everyone in the path?

The tree that God has planted doesn't have to worry when heat comes. It has leaves—green leaves—to shield and nourish it. And the Spirit desires to shade you from the heat of anger as he nurtures your life in Christ. Listen to the apostle James:

Wherefore, my beloved brethren, let every man be swift to hear, slow to speak, slow to wrath: For the wrath of man worketh not the righteousness of God. (James 1:19–20)

What does a tree do to shade itself and to find nourishment during the heat of summer days? It "clothes" itself with leaves. Branches bloom and leaves blossom, not simply to make the tree stately and beautiful, but for shade, for sustenance, and to provide a mechanism by which it can constantly exchange bad for good, carbon dioxide for oxygen.

Of course, God "clothes" the trees with leaves. He creates and preserves all things. And your Maker has also promised to clothe you by his grace with his righteous life. He shows compassion, kindness, humility, gentleness, patience, and forgiveness to you in Christ's cross. This mercy then makes it possible for you to work through your anger, release your anger, and express your anger—when that's appropriate—in a healthy, constructive way. He will put on you the new nature of your life in Christ.

Angry today? Ask your Father to help you trust him to guide and protect you through the heat.

Deeper and Higher

Contemplate the stately beauty of God's love flowing through you as you think about Paul's concluding words in Colossians:

And above all these things put on charity,
which is the bond of perfectness.
Colossians 3:14

Welcome Back

For he is our peace, who hath made both one, and hath broken down the middle wall of partition between us; Having abolished in his flesh the enmity, even the law of commandments contained in ordinances; for to make in himself of twain one new man, so making peace; And that he might reconcile both unto God in one body by the cross. (Ephesians 2:14–16)

The hot, harmful breath of conflict blows all too frequently through relationships. Perhaps through yours, too. Perhaps even today, you have experienced a painful disagreement. Or maybe

it was worse than that; maybe it was a fierce, agonizing fight with someone you work with, someone you live with, or someone you usually sit close to in church. You've parted ways. You've stopped talking. You have no plans and you foresee no reason, no reason ever, to make contact or to seek reconciliation.

Jesus told a story about a prodigal son who realized his mistake. The boy knew he was wrong. He knew he had hurt his dad. But he trusted that his father would forgive and welcome him home.

This son wanted what we all want—reconciliation with the Father who gives us life and breath. So first he spoke to his own heart: "I will arise and go to my father, and will say unto

him, Father, I have sinned against heaven, and before thee"
(Luke 15:18).

Reconciliation begins with a step: *I will arise.* When the heat of
conflict lingers in your life, take the first step: "Father, I have
sinned against heaven, and before thee." Ask your Father's
forgiveness. He has reconciled you in his Son and will welcome
you home again and again to his mercy in your Lord Jesus.

Then step toward others. Ask your Father to give you strength.
Call on him for wisdom to know where, how, to go forward.
Pray that he opens a door . . . for the relationship to be restored
and renewed.

Trust his Word: You are like a tree planted by water. You need
not fear the heat of this day, for in Christ your leaves are green.

Deeper and Higher

Listen tenderly, obediently to the Father's appeal:

Now then we are ambassadors for Christ,
as though God did beseech you by us:
we pray you in Christ's stead,
be ye reconciled to God.

2 Corinthians 5:20

Days 20&21

Pressure to . . .

During these next two days, reflect on the different ways God is working in you so that you may stand firm in Christ throughout all seasons of your life.

Conform to This World
Dominate Others
Satisfy Personal Desires
Lose Control
Prolong Conflict

Blessed is the man that trusteth in the LORD, and whose hope the LORD is. For he shall be as a tree planted by the waters, and that spreadeth out her roots by the river, and shall not see when heat cometh, but her leaf shall be green.
Jeremiah 17:7–8

Blessed is the man that trusteth in the L<small>ORD</small>, and whose hope the L<small>ORD</small> is. For he shall be as a tree planted by the waters, and that spreadeth out her roots by the river, and shall not see when heat cometh, but her leaf shall be green; and shall not be careful in the year of drought, neither shall cease from yielding fruit.
Jeremiah 17:7–8

God has planted you
  for the dry spells every man faces.

Though you feel parched and drained at times,
  don't be anxious:
  you are not alone.

Your Lord has watered you with his Word
  and supplies his wisdom
  and strength for you to be a man of faith.

He will rain down his grace on you,
  growing you deeper and higher,
  that you may be richly satisfied
  as you put your trust in him.

Living Water

Jesus answered and said unto her, Whosoever drinketh of this water shall thirst again: But whosoever drinketh of the water that I shall give him shall never thirst; but the water that I shall give him shall be in him a well of water springing up into everlasting life. (John 4:13–14)

In a year of drought, Jeremiah assures us, the man of faith has no worries. This prophet knew firsthand the bleak reality of dry, desolate days. At one point in his mission to God's people, Jeremiah received a word from the Lord "concerning the dearth" that ravaged his nation (Jeremiah 14:1). The nation's pain was real; tears and pleas for mercy flowed from the people of Judah as they suffered from lack of water, lack of food, and lack of hope.

In times of drought still today, we have every *human* reason to be anxious, because water is life and life is fragile. We have reason to be anxious, that is, unless we drink continually from the water that Jesus gives. That water is *living* water.

Are you thirsty, dried out, anxious? Jesus offers you a drink—a long, satisfying drink from a spring that wells up to eternal life. In him you have no lasting drought, no permanent lack, because he can and freely does pour out living water to refresh you, even in your driest, most desolate days.

The tree God has planted you to be "shall not be careful in the year of drought," Jeremiah assures you. Not that you'll escape drought conditions in your life. Not that you'll always steer clear of those arid, seemingly barren patches every man faces.

Notice exactly what the prophet says: you shall not be careful—no ultimate, permanent worries. You'll stand firm and tall in the confidence that your Father has called you by name and chosen you to be a man who lives by faith. You can trust his promise to work in you and through you to bear the fruit of the Spirit in all the seasons of your life.

When dry, desolate days overtake you, drink deeply. Drink often. Drink the water that Jesus pours out for you.

Deeper and Higher
Ask the Spirit to refresh you as Christ has promised:

If any man thirst, let him come unto me,
and drink. He that believeth on me,
as the scripture hath said, out of his belly
shall flow rivers of living water.
John 7:37–38

Day 23

Thirsty for God

O God, thou art my God; early will I seek thee: my soul thirsteth for thee, my flesh longeth for thee in a dry and thirsty land, where no water is. (Psalm 63:1)

Trees suffer in drought. Even mature, resilient trees are affected by prolonged dry weather. Leaves and bark show early signs of deprivation. Prolonged drought can take a severe toll on the hardiest of oaks and pines and maples. Trunk rings prove it.

In Psalm 63, David compares the hurt he's feeling to a time of prolonged drought. Alone, in the desert, he had no one to turn to, no one to hold onto. He felt loss. He felt lost. He describes his longing for water where none may be found. Thirsty to the roots of his being, David was desperate for God to plant him beside the water, to irrigate him with a Father's life-giving presence.

Deep hurt makes us thirst in this same way. We ache for something that will dampen the pain. We long for even a moment's relief. We yearn for someone who knows how to diminish our grief, just a little.

You may have been touched by hurt and loss. You can still see events playing out: In your own home. Or on the job. Or in your doctor's office. Like David, you're thirsty inside. Like David, you long for water, for something to turn to and hold onto in the dry and dreary land you've entered.

From his desert place, David said to his Father, "My soul followeth hard after thee: thy right hand upholdeth me" (Psalm 63:8). From your own desert place right now, you can trust this same truth. Now's the time to grab hold of your Father's life-giving presence. Now's the time to tighten your grip on his promises. Repeat King David's words to your King Jesus:

Lord, you are my God; I seek you in my hurt. My soul thirsts for your compassion; my body longs for your healing touch. I cling to you, Lord. Hold me tightly in your gracious hands.

Deeper and Higher
Now confess this truth with David:

Because thy lovingkindness is better than life,
my lips shall praise thee.
Thus will I bless thee while I live:
I will lift up my hands in thy name.

Psalm 63:3–4

Balanced and Whole

The righteous shall flourish like the palm tree: he shall grow like a cedar in Lebanon. (Psalm 92:12)

Tough and fragrant. It's an unusual combination. Yet in biblical times cedar wood was prized for both its durability and its sweet smell. Merchants and craftsmen tapped cedars for resins and oils and then produced anointments and perfumes. Solomon bartered with the king of Tyre for cedars from Lebanon. He devoted the wood, with its rich finish and long-lasting aroma, to building the Lord's temple (1 Kings 5).

Through his prophet Hosea, the Lord calls Israel a "cedar." He sees his people as both tough and fragrant. He's planted them. He's caused their roots to spread out deep and wide. He sees in his people the splendor of an olive tree, highly valued in the ancient world as a symbol of peace and happiness. He's fashioned his beloved son Israel like a "cedar," because this provides a perfect combination of qualities to accomplish his will and purposes.

What combination—usual, interesting, or suitable—is the Lord planting in you? Your Father may desire to give your life balance. He may want to work in you a symmetry, a harmony and consistency you may need in the future as you serve him. Perhaps he's building in you deep conviction, tempered by compassion. Or perhaps passion, moderated by patience.

No matter what the mix you need, your Father knows how to balance you, how to water and cultivate just exactly the gifts you need.

Some traits, some qualities may lie dormant right now. You may need a soaking rain and healthy nutrients from God's Word to enable you to finish a project with excellence or make a positive impression on a client or manager. Whatever you lack for the work and witness to which your Father has called you, he will provide. He is growing you into a mighty cedar—valuable, balanced, and whole. He will grant you wisdom and give you all you need to "bear fruit" in abundance, for his glory and your good.

Deeper and Higher
As you call on your God, take comfort in his reply:

I am like a green fir tree.
From me is thy fruit found.
Hosea 14:8

Free and Flexible

For though I be free from all men, yet have I made myself servant unto all, that I might gain the more. To the weak became I as weak, that I might gain the weak: I am made all things to all men, that I might by all means save some. And this I do for the gospel's sake, that I might be partaker thereof with you. (1 Corinthians 9:19, 22–23)

The trunk of a tree rarely moves. But branches do. Branches move daily as they are touched by gentle breezes and swayed by gusty winds. Branches dip and bend when feathery robins huddle in winter and plump squirrels frolic in summer. Branches are the "give-and-take" part of trees. Bouncing and swaying, branches and their leaves are poetry in motion—trees on the move.

Paul considered himself a man on the move, a branch connected to the Tree of Life. Literally, he traveled thousands of miles to share the Good News of Christ. Figuratively, he moved daily—sometimes subtly, sometimes dramatically—among all kinds of people. Jews and Gentiles. Slaves and rich merchants. Government officials and greedy swindlers. He could dip and bend to accommodate new settings and specific needs.

But the "trunk" of his faith never moved. He never compromised on God's Word. He was free and flexible in his ministry, but immovable on the saving truth of the Gospel. By his candid admission, he gives and takes, all for "the gospel's sake," that by grace he might share the Lord's infinite blessings with many others.

The tree that God has made you to be stands free and flexible. You're released from sin, the fear of death, and the power of the devil. Jesus has unshackled you and planted you in his love. And he allows you to live in the "give-and-take" of his Gospel, to become, under his leadership, "all things to all men." You're free to move forward, even in a drought, as you bear fruit in all your relationships.

Put your anxiety behind you today. See the doors your Father opens. Walk through, trusting his guidance.

Deeper and Higher
Meditate on God's exhortation:

See then that ye walk circumspectly,
not as fools, but as wise, Redeeming
the time, because the days are evil.
Wherefore be ye not unwise,
but understanding what the
will of the Lord is.
Ephesians 5:15–17

Fruitful Branches

I am the true vine, and my Father is the husbandman.
Every branch in me that beareth not fruit he taketh away:
and every branch that beareth fruit, he purgeth it, that it may
bring forth more fruit. (John 15:1–2)

It's no surprise that the prophets, apostles, and our Lord himself
all speak often about fruit, about fruitful trees and branches.
Almond, apricot, date, fig, olive, and pomegranate trees and
shrubs provided groceries for every family during Bible times.
Branches laden with fruit played a vital economic role in each
village marketplace and in many industries—farming,
manufacturing, international trade.

Ask a fruit grower, and he'll affirm the Bible's deep insight.
The process of growth in orchard and garden mirrors that
process in many other dimensions, the spiritual realm in
particular. In the Upper Room that Thursday evening before
his death, Jesus used a familiar picture of fruit-bearing to
convey profound truths about true discipleship:

Abide in me, and I in you. As the branch cannot bear fruit
of itself, except it abide in the vine; no more can ye,
except ye abide in me. (John 15:4)

Jesus is the "true vine," the trunk of the tree the Father has
planted. He is the genuine, permanent, eternal Son of God.
You are his branch. He has saved you, grafted you into his saving
death and resurrection.

His selfless act of sacrifice, his death on the tree of the cross in payment for each one of your sins, has sown new life in you. Now your Father, the true gardener, is filling that life with buds and then with abundant, generous, and luscious fruit, pruning you as he sees fit, to make you even more fruitful.

In every season, even during the dry spells, you trust your Father to make your fruit grow. And you have the privilege of asking, "Make me more fruitful!"

Deeper and Higher
Hear the Living Vine again:

I am the vine, ye are the branches:
He that abideth in me, and I in him,
the same bringeth forth much fruit:
for without me ye can do nothing.
John 15:5

The Dry Spells

*During the next two days, reflect on the different ways
God is working in you so that you may stand firm in
Christ through all the seasons of your life.*

My Lord's Living Water
Hurt and Loss
Balance
Flexibility
Fruitful Branches

*Blessed is the man that trusteth in the LORD, and whose hope the
LORD is. For he shall be as a tree planted by the waters, and that
spreadeth out her roots by the river, and shall not see when heat
cometh, but her leaf shall be green; and shall not be careful in the
year of drought, neither shall cease from yielding fruit.*
Jeremiah 17:7–8

*Blessed is the man that trusteth in the LORD, and whose hope
the LORD is. For he shall be as a tree planted by the waters,
and that spreadeth out her roots by the river, and shall not
see when heat cometh, but her leaf shall be green;
and shall not be careful in the year of drought,
neither shall cease from yielding fruit.*
Jeremiah 17:7–8

God truly has planted you.

And he will tend you and harvest your fruit
all the days of your life.

He will bless you and keep you.

He will make his face shine on you to make you grow
deeper and higher
as you follow your Lord and Savior.

Trust him. He is your faithful God.

A Blessed Man

Blessed is the man that walketh not in the counsel of the ungodly, nor standeth in the way of sinners, nor sitteth in the seat of the scornful. . . . And he shall be like a tree planted by the rivers of water, that bringeth forth his fruit in his season; his leaf also shall not wither. (Psalm 1:1, 3)

Sound familiar? Jeremiah was not the only biblical writer to portray the man of faith as a tree planted by water.

The book of Psalms begins on a note that echoes through all the other 149 songs, poems, and prayers that follow. Psalm 1 sets the tone, points the way, making a bold foundational statement. If we were to paraphrase, we might say, "Blessed is the man in a living faith relationship with the Lord."

Jeremiah agrees! His words have now become familiar: *Blessed is the man that trusteth in the LORD and whose hope the LORD is.*

Consider yourself blessed today. Planted by God. Green in the summer's heat. Fruitful even in the dry season. Jeremiah's faithful words describe you, a man loved by God, called by God, equipped by God, and sent forth to serve your God.

But know that *blessed* means much more than "staying cool under fire." To be blessed means more than merely enjoying the multiplication of possessions, status, position, or authority. Jeremiah follows all of Scripture in using the word *blessed* to mean primarily enjoying a relationship of favor with the Lord himself:

> *Blessed is he*
> > *whose transgression is forgiven,*
> > *whose sin is covered.*
> *Blessed is the man*
> > *unto whom the L*ORD *imputeth not iniquity,*
> > *and in whose spirit there is no guile.*
> > > *(Psalm 32:1–2)*

God looks on you as his very own son—what a blessing!
He regards you as forgiven and blameless—what a blessing!
Speaking from his heart, he declares you holy and perfect in
the cross of Jesus Christ—what a blessing!

You belong to God himself as his very own chosen possession.
He's seated you with Christ in his glory and given you authority
to serve in his name.

You are a blessed man . . . a man of faith!

Deeper and Higher
Another psalm of trust to remember:

But I am like a green olive tree
in the house of God:
I trust in the mercy
of God for ever
and ever.
> Psalm 52:8

My Health and Salvation

And he shewed me a pure river of water of life, clear as crystal, proceeding out of the throne of God and of the Lamb. In the midst of the street of it, and on either side of the river, was there the tree of life, which bare twelve manner of fruits, and yielded her fruit every month: and the leaves of the tree were for the healing of the nations. (Revelation 22:1–2)

Trees suggest many wonderful associations in the Bible. One is health and healing. As John's vision in the book of Revelation draws to a close, he sees the tree of life—Christ's own planting in his eternal kingdom—bestow healing on all who trust him for salvation. No more pain, no more suffering, no more death in the heavenly city. The Lamb of God makes all things new.

God regards your own health and healing with fatherly concern. He encourages you to manage your body, mind, and spirit as a steward of his gifts. And when your health falters and you need healing, he invites you to ask for his goodness and mercy, according to his will in Christ. In sickness or in health, he calls you to trust in him.

Your Lord holds your well-being in his hands. Man of faith, listen! Take to heart your Savior's promise in Ezekiel 17:22–24:

Thus saith the Lord GOD:

*I will also take of the highest branch of the high cedar, and will
set it; I will crop off from the top of his young twigs a tender one,
and will plant it upon an high mountain and eminent. . . .*
(He means you.)

*In the mountain of the height of Israel will I plant it: and it shall
bring forth boughs, and bear fruit, and be a goodly cedar. . . .*
(The Lord will make you effective where he plants you.)

*And under it shall dwell all fowl of every wing; in the shadow
of the branches thereof shall they dwell. . . .* (He'll make you
a blessing to others, and you'll share cheerfully from
your abundance.)

*And all the trees of the field shall know that I the LORD have
brought down the high tree, have exalted the low tree, have dried
up the green tree, and have made the dry tree to flourish. . . .*
(Everyone will know that your Father orders all your days.)

Deeper and Higher
Attention, please:

I the LORD have spoken and have done it.
Ezekiel 17:24

My Joy and Praise

*Let the heavens rejoice, and let the
earth be glad; let the sea roar, and
the fulness thereof. Let the field be
joyful, and all that is therein: then
shall all the trees of the wood rejoice.
(Psalm 96:11–12)*

God convenes a grand celebration
for his creation. The heavens are
present; earth's accounted for. The
sea joins in. The fields wouldn't
miss it for the world.

Who leads the singing? *The trees!*

Can you imagine the resonant
bass tones that the mighty oaks
contribute to the chorus? Can
you hear the balsams joining in
as tenors? From all around the
earth the voices blend together . . .
cherry trees and chestnuts,
hawthorns and hickories, pear trees
and poplars . . . all in joyful
praise to their Lord!

You, too, are a tree planted to
worship. You have the right and the
duty to raise your voice, united with
the chorus that sings praise to the

one and only Creator. And the melody you add is the song of the church, the song of thousands upon thousands, ten thousand times ten thousand, who worship the Father, the Son, and the Holy Spirit:

Worthy is the Lamb that was slain to receive power, and riches, and wisdom, and strength, and honour, and glory, and blessing. And every creature which is in heaven, and on the earth, and under the earth, and such as are in the sea, and all that are in them, heard I saying, Blessing, and honour, and glory, and power, be unto him that sitteth upon the throne, and unto the Lamb for ever and ever. (Revelation 5:12–13)

Your Father summons you to praise. By his design, you are invited to the grand celebration each week. Sunday, Wednesday, Saturday— whenever you gather with God's people to lift your voice in thanksgiving, to hear his Word, and to sink your roots more deeply into the fertile soil of his Good News.

As a man of faith, take seriously the Lord's call to worship. Set an example for your family . . . for the children in your life . . . for your friends who may at times waver in their commitment to their local church family. Join in the song: "Worthy is the Lamb!"

Deeper and Higher
As a tree of God's planting, picture this as you
prepare to celebrate:

For ye shall go out with joy, and be led forth with peace: the mountains and the hills shall break forth before you into singing, and all the trees of the field shall clap their hands.

Isaiah 55:12

My Days and Years

Remember the former things of old: for I am God, and there is none else; I am God, and there is none like me, Declaring the end from the beginning, and from ancient times the things that are not yet done. (Isaiah 46:9–10)

Over 1,500 years. That's the age of some sequoias!

Sequoia trees are perhaps the most fascinating trees in North America. Located in the coastal regions of California and Oregon, sequoias tower over all other species of trees. They can grow to a height of over 300 feet. Their trunks range from 10 to 20 feet in diameter. Nothing else really compares. These "giants" of the earth stand proud and tall as testaments to the God who reigns from everlasting to everlasting.

Yet sequoias only dimly reflect the reality of the grandeur that blazes from Isaiah's words: *I am God, and there is none else; I am God, and there is none like me.*

The Lord God commands time. He controls days and years. He makes beginnings. He chooses endings. From birth to death, all creation, including the lofty sequoia, lies in his hands, dependent on his care. He orders and sustains all life, from the dense forests of northern California to the wild sapling of a fig tree near Jerusalem. There is none like God.

This same God also directs your time on earth. Hear his word of grandeur directed to you personally: I am *your* God. No other. I am *your* God. This God, your God, knows every beginning you'll have. He chooses when to bring to a close all your plans. The Father who has planted you and guided you throughout your life down to this very day calls you as a witness to his everlasting reign.

So let his Word blaze in your heart. Believe what he has said in the Bible. Put it into practice. Continue to grow up into the very stature of Christ himself (Ephesians 4:13). You will loom as a "giant" of faith, and the people around you will take courage in the God to whom your life testifies. Incomparable . . .

Deeper and Higher

Trust the Lord's unshakable decree:

My counsel shall stand, and I will do all my pleasure: Calling a ravenous bird from the east, the man that executeth my counsel from a far country: yea, I have spoken it, I will also bring it to pass; I have purposed it, I will also do it.

Isaiah 46:10–11

My Focus

That I may know him, and the power of his resurrection, and the fellowship of his sufferings, being made conformable unto his death; If by any means I might attain unto the resurrection of the dead. (Philippians 3:10–11)

Having read the devotions in this booklet, you know the prophet Jeremiah a bit better than when you began. You know what he believed about God. You know what he cherished about faith and living in this world. But above all, you know he wants *all men* to know the living Lord.

To the day he died, Jeremiah remained focused on that. Perhaps as he closed his eyes for the last time on this earth, his final thoughts returned to the phrase he had proclaimed throughout his ministry: *Blessed is the man that trusteth in the LORD, and whose hope the LORD is.*

Jeremiah was focused. He knew where his real life began and where it would end. God wants you, too, to have a clear focus for your life:

> To know Christ . . .
> the power of his *resurrection*
> the fellowship of sharing in his *sufferings*
> becoming like him in his *death*
> attaining to the *resurrection* from the dead.

The beginning of your real life is Christ's suffering, his death. By faith you are a partner, a "fellow" in his sacrifice for the sins of the world.

The ending of your real life is Christ's resurrection, his victory over death. His resurrection is power, God's power for you! By faith in his matchless triumph, you are assured of your own resurrection when Jesus comes back in glory.

He is the Lord you trust. In Jesus, and in Jesus alone, you've placed your confidence. Like Jeremiah, you have a focus, every day, through every planting and replanting, through times of heat and drought, through opportunities and setbacks. You are a man of faith. Now grow deeper and higher . . .

- Send your roots out, far and wide.
- Stand tall against the heat, in the drought.
- Drink deeply from the Living Water.
- And let the Spirit's fruit mature in you.

Deeper and Higher
Focus on this tree . . . always:

Who his own self bare our sins in his own body on the tree, that we, being dead to sins, should live unto righteousness: by whose stripes ye were healed.
1 Peter 2:24

The Man Who Trusts the Lord

*During these next two days, reflect on the different ways
God will work in your life to keep you a man of faith.*

A Blessed Man
My Health and Salvation
My Joy and Praise
My Days and Years
My Focus

*Blessed is the man that trusteth in the LORD, and whose hope
the LORD is. For he shall be as a tree planted by the waters,
and that spreadeth out her roots by the river, and shall not
see when heat cometh, but her leaf shall be green;
and shall not be careful in the year of drought,
neither shall cease from yielding fruit.*
Jeremiah 17:7–8

If this book has made a
difference in your life or
if you have simply enjoyed
it, we would like to hear
from you. Your words
will encourage us!
You can reach us at:
Editorial Dept., CTA, Inc.,
1625 Larkin Williams Rd.,
Fenton, MO 63026-1205
or by e-mail at
editor@CTAinc.com.

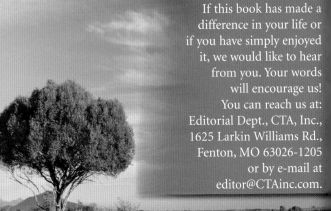